PATH

A guide to the practice of silent prayer

by
Fr Paul Nicholson SJ

All booklets are published thanks to the generous support of the members of the Catholic Truth Society

CATHOLIC TRUTH SOCIETY
PUBLISHERS TO THE HOLY SEE

CONTENTS

 First published 2017 by The Incorporated Catholic Truth Society, 40-46 Harleyford Road London SE11 5AY Tel: 020 7640 0042 Fax: 020 7640 0046.

ISBN 978 1 78469 174 5

INTRODUCTION

"Lord, teach us to pray", Jesus's disciples ask him halfway through St Luke's gospel. What happens next is significant. Jesus doesn't offer them a workshop on methods of prayer, or a detailed explanation of techniques. He gives them a formula, a set pattern of words, and instructs them "Say this when you pray". And his followers have been doing that ever since, day by day through twenty centuries, approaching God with the words "Our Father..."

Many of us will have first learnt to pray like this. For Roman Catholics, the Our Father, the Hail Mary and the Glory Be are three set prayers learnt, perhaps literally, at your mother's knee. Later come the prayers of the Mass, the Gloria and the Creed. Other Christian traditions will share some of these, and have their own favoured prayers. Reciting these, and reflecting on the meaning of the well-worn words, can take you a long way in the spiritual life.

There comes a time, though, when many people find that this is no longer enough to sustain them. Maybe the words lose their meaning, or seem to get in the way between myself coming to prayer, and the God whom I hope to meet there. For some at this point, substituting my own words instead of those I have long known may be enough. Talking to God "just as one friend talks to another" (the phrase comes from St Ignatius of Loyola, founder of the Jesuits) breathes new life into my prayer, and deepens my relationship with Christ. Others though may find themselves drawn in a different direction, to fewer words rather than more. In a busy and noisy world, perhaps silence is the place to discover what God might be wanting to communicate to me.

In 2010 BBC television decided to test this out. With the help of Fr Christopher Jamison, then Abbot of Worth Abbey in Sussex, they first took half-a-dozen volunteers to experience the silence characteristic of a large part of monastic life. Later in the series, entitled *The Great Silence*, the group were invited to visit St Beuno's, a Jesuit-run retreat house in north Wales, to engage in a six-day silent retreat. How would they react to this unfamiliar setting? Would they, in truth, find themselves drawn closer to God as a result?

It was clear that each of the participants was entering into the experience with a certain degree of nervousness. What would it be like, having to be silent for so long? What would there be to do? How would they spend the time, when so many of the things that filled their everyday lives (family, friends, work, TV and radio, the internet, newspapers, music) were, temporarily, taken away? Behind this lay an idea of silence as empty, purposeless and even threatening. Yet each one of them discovered, during their days of retreat, that something important happened to them precisely because they were in silence. It was as if once many of the common daily distractions were removed, they found themselves better able to focus on what is more important in life. And as that focus sharpened, long-desired changes became possible.

It's fair to ask whether this kind of experience is only available to those able to afford the time and expense of going away to a remote spirituality centre for days or weeks at a time. The good news is that the answer to that question is "No"! Most of us are able, with a little guidance and encouragement, to carve out a small amount of time – quarter of an hour, 30 minutes – now and again when we can be quiet. It might be early in the morning, before the busy-ness of the day begins; or a few minutes' winding down, last thing at night. You might find your quiet time lying in a warm bath, or when you take the dog for a walk. Certainly, you might need to work at discovering a suitable pause within the day, and safeguarding it from distractions or the interference of other people. But the chances are that, with a bit of effort, you'll be able to arrive at a time that works for you.

Finding time, though, is only half the battle. Once you have come to a time of quiet, what do you do then? If you're not simply to stare aimlessly at a blank wall, how can you profitably spend this period you've set aside? What follows in this booklet is a range of answers to this question. They are cast in the form of "exercises", things to do in order to reach a desired goal. Just as, if you want to get fit, you might give some time to jogging, swimming or using the machines in a gym, so if you want to focus on those questions that are most important in your life, the exercises that follow can help you. Some are more general: letting the silence itself grow deeper, or trying a wide-ranging review of the pattern of your life. Others are more specific: how to deal with hurtful memories, or notice again the good things of a single day. All alike make good use of silence, and all can be returned to time and again to look more fully at what they are revealing.

Each of these exercises is presented as a prayerful reflection. Feel entirely free to pick and choose between them, using whatever you find helpful and leaving aside anything that doesn't seem to work for you. These exercises are no more than tools to help you to communicate more fully with God. It is important to realise that I am not alone in looking over my life. I carry out this process in the company of a loving God who looks with me, supports me and may well have something to add to my own reflections. Some may find this off-putting. Is this a hidden way of persuading me to go to church, or sign up to the belief-system of a particular sect or church? This is another question that can be answered with a firm "No"! The Twelve Step programmes, of which Alcoholics Anonymous is perhaps the best known, ask their members to work with the idea of a "power greater than ourselves", which many call God. Their programmes can work with whatever idea those undertaking them feel comfortable using. So, too, with these exercises. If you have any idea of God at all, use that as you start here. Even if you have no particular idea, looking at whatever most brings you to life, or fills you with energy, can have a similar effect.

The trick with an exercise is to do it. No amount of reading fitness programmes, trying on different trainers at a local sports shop or watching athletes competing on TV, is going to make me more fit. I actually have to go out there and jog, swim or lift the weights. The same is true of the exercises that follow. No amount of reading about them, thinking them through, or putting them off until tomorrow, will lead you more deeply into what is most important in your own life just now. So, if you're ready to make that journey, I invite you simply to turn the page and start.

EXERCISE ONE: PATHWAYS INTO SILENCE

One of the things that frequently gets in the way of prayer and reflection is a lack of quiet and stillness, inside and outside of myself. I can perhaps do something about the outside noise: choose a quiet place, switch the phone off, pick a time when I am less likely to be disturbed. But what of interior stillness and silence? How do I stop my mind racing off in a dozen different directions, throwing up all sorts of distractions which come between me and God?

Taking a few minutes to try one or other of these stillness exercises as I start my prayer can be very helpful in this regard. Sometimes this may be a preparation for another kind of prayer. At other times, simply entering into a companionable silence with God may be all the prayer I want and need.

Awareness of my body

Start by sitting in a relaxed position, with your back straight, feet side by side on the floor, and your hands resting gently on your lap.

Concentrate for a moment on becoming aware of the feel of your feet as they press against the floor. Notice the feel of the ground beneath them, any constriction of your footwear, the feel of your individual toes – you might need to wiggle them a little to do this!

Now let that point of awareness travel up into your lower legs. Flex the muscles, and be aware of how this part of your body feels. Let any tension you find there relax and flow away.

Let that point of awareness move slowly round your body, gently travelling from one part to the next. Notice the feeling in each place, and let any tension ebb away before moving on.

When your point of awareness has reached your head and face, and spent some time there, let it return to your feet, and slowly make the same journey again, releasing any tension initially overlooked, or that has built up since you last focused there.

When this process feels as if it has reached a natural conclusion, let that point of awareness come to rest somewhere at the centre of yourself, and remain there quietly.

Awareness of sounds

Start by sitting in a relaxed position, with your back straight, feet side by side on the floor, and your hands resting gently on your lap.

Take a few moments to focus on any sounds you can hear outside the room where you are sitting. Try to identify each, and for a moment or two focus on that one alone.

Without trying to block out those sounds (let them be!) let your attention move inwards, to any sounds you can hear within the room where you are – the ticking of a clock, the hum of electrical appliances, etc. For a few moments, let your whole attention be on these sounds.

Again, without blocking these out, let your point of attention take another step inwards, and be aware of all the "noise" going on within yourself. This may be physical (the sound of your own breathing), or may be an awareness of the rush of thoughts and feelings passing through your heart and mind.

Finally, take one further step inwards, and let your awareness come to rest in some quiet, still place in the centre of yourself. Rest there in the quiet for as long as seems good to you.

Awareness of my breathing

Start by sitting in a relaxed position, with your back straight, feet side by side on the floor, and your hands resting gently on your lap.

Slowly let yourself become aware of the pattern of your own breathing. Notice whether it is deep or shallow, regular or irregular, through your mouth or your nose or both.

Don't try and change or control your breathing. Just notice as you breathe in, and as you breathe out.

(If there is anything in this experience that bothers you, if your breath starts coming too fast, for example, gently leave this exercise aside and move to one of the other stillness exercises.)

You may want simply to rest in the quietness that this awareness of breathing leads to. If, however, you want this exercise to develop into more explicit prayer, the following ideas may help:

- As you breathe in, feel yourself drawing God's life-giving Spirit deep inside yourself, so that the Spirit fills the whole of your being.
- As you breathe out, release anything that would tend to separate you from God, or get in the way between yourself and God.

EXERCISE TWO: REFLECTING ON THE DAY

"I don't know where today went", people often say. In our busy lives, it's easy for hours, days, even whole weeks to go by without really registering with us. This exercise is aimed at making you more aware of what went on during a day (or whatever period of time you choose to review). It sees the events of that time as a series of gifts, and invites you to notice more fully your response to being gifted in this way.

Take some time to become still, finding whatever quietness you can around you and within you. Use any method you find helpful for this. You might find that one or other of the three techniques in Exercise 1 above is helpful to you here.

Enter the prayer with an attitude of gratitude, realising anew that all you have and are comes as a gift from God.

Ask for God's light as you review the period of time you want to look at, that God will show you what has been most significant.

Let your mind's eye look back over the time, gently noticing whatever catches your attention. There is no need to work hard at recalling every moment – let what will emerge. This may be rather like a film of the time you're considering slowly playing again as you watch.

Notice particularly moments of life, of light, of energy; and moments when these seemed drained. What was your response at the time? How would you want to respond to God now as you notice them again?

Speak to God "as one friend speaks to another" about what you have noticed in the prayer.

End by looking ahead, and in the light of what you have seen, ask God for the gifts and graces you need for the time immediately ahead.

EXERCISE THREE: REVIEWING YOUR LIFE JOURNEY

This prayer exercise invites you to look back over your life journey in order to let God enable you to recognise more clearly the ways in which God has been with you at all the different moments. If Exercise 2 offered a snapshot of God's work on a given day, this exercise is more like a feature film, with its own plot and characters.

First take some time to become still and quiet, using an awareness exercise (such as those in Exercise 1) or any other way into prayer that you know from experience works well for you.

Then ask God to awaken in you during this period of prayer the gift of remembering, bring to mind in you whatever it would be good for you to notice.

Now simply let the "landscape" of your life unfold before your mind's eye, and let your attention roam where it will within that landscape.

The following questions may help you in your reflection:

- Where have been the special moments in your life's journey so far, the milestones and the mountain-tops (events, people, places…)? What gifts was God giving you in these times?

- What about the valleys and the deserts – times of darkness, pain, or confusion? Where is the Lord in these? Where has God seemed absent?

- Where have you come to cross-roads, rivers to cross, a choice of paths – places of decision or crisis? How has God guided you in these times?

Draw a "map" of your journey, in whatever way you like. You might want to use a picture, or words, or symbols – make use of whatever is most meaningful to you.

Spend some time sharing your memories and your map with God – let the Spirit lead you here.

Finally, as you stand again in the present moment, what might you need to ask God for to help you move forward on your journey?

EXERCISE FOUR: DISCERNMENT – CHOOSING WHAT IS LIFE-GIVING

Discernment is the name given to a form of prayerful reflection that seeks to know more fully the will of God in my own life, or the life of a group to which I belong. The will of God is not some kind of static, hidden blueprint, to which I must conform. It is rather an invitation to live creatively, using my God-given gifts and talents in a way that allows me to be most fully the person I truly am, the person God has created me to be.

Discernment happens at the point where head and heart come together. It involves doing my homework – what is the actual issue here, what are my options, have I a realistic sense of my strengths and weaknesses? It also calls me to take the time to discover how I really feel about the question, at a deep level, where I find myself most drawn.

Above all, discernment involves a choice between options which are good – I do not discern whether I should become a bank-robber or kidnapper or not! – and is carried out in confidence that God will still be with me, whichever choice I make.

One Christian tradition speaks of three moments when discernment may take place.

First, there are times when I simply know what it is that I should do, without any doubt entering in. I may or may not be able to give convincing reasons for my choice. But I could not take another path and be true to myself.

Second, there are times when, faced with possible paths ahead, I find myself greatly stirred up at the level of my feelings. I may be greatly drawn to one alternative and repelled by another. Or my feelings may see-saw back and forth as I consider the options over time.

Third, I may approach the decisions I have to make in an unruffled state, finding that I can view the different possibilities with their different reasons calmly, without great movements of feelings in any particular direction.

In this understanding, the ideal is where the feelings (second approach above) and the intellect (third) pull in the same direction. In authentic cases of the first kind of discernment, there is no problem. Even here, though, it is worth checking out the responses of heart and head so that I do not get carried along by a blind enthusiasm.

The following prayer exercise brings together the different elements of the discernment process, and gives time for me to note the direction that they incline me towards.

I begin this prayerful reflection by taking time to become still, outwardly and inwardly, and asking for God to show me in this prayer what it would be useful for me to see.

Next I spell out for myself as clearly as I can what my real options are in the situation which I am trying to discern.

What is the actual question that I am facing, and what are the concrete alternatives?

I then map out, using four columns, the two sides of each of two alternatives that I want to explore. For example, if I am trying to decide between teaching in the UK and voluntary work overseas, the columns would look like this:

Advantages in UK teaching	Disadvantages in UK teaching	Advantages to overseas voluntary work	Disadvantages to overseas voluntary work

I spend time filling in whatever comes to mind for each of these columns. Then I take some time to sit and see how I feel about each option as I look at what I have written. If I have time, I spend a while imagining that I have opted one way or the other. What does that make me feel like?

If the matter is now clear, or I have no more time before I have to decide, I make a decision based on what I have seen and entrust it to God. Otherwise, I may choose to come back to this prayer at a later date. Either way, I draw the prayer to a close, perhaps noting anything significant here.

EXERCISE FIVE: KEEPING A REFLECTIVE JOURNAL

"There are many other signs that Jesus worked and the disciples saw, but they are not recorded in this book. These are recorded so that you may believe..." (*Jn* 20:30-31)

Keeping a reflective prayer journal can be a great aid towards growth in the spiritual life. Over time it offers a record of experiences that you have had, and what you have made of them as they happened. This means that looking back it becomes easier to see how and where you have changed, in outlook or in patterns of behaviour. Such changes are often so slow and almost imperceptible that they can easily go unnoticed.

It is good to notice what such a journal is not. It is not simply a diary, recording in more or less detail the events of each day. It is not a list of things to do, or of tasks accomplished. Nor is it a record of the books you've read, the films you've watched or the insights that have occurred to you. Yet it may contain elements of all of these.

One way of understanding what to record in such a journal is to ask yourself: "What has stirred me up, has moved me, over the period that I am considering?" This puts you in touch with what Ignatius Loyola would call "movements of spirits", and which he saw as being indicators of God at work in a person's life. What has moved you might be a conversation you have had; a book that you've read; a situation that you have encountered; a piece of work that you have done; etc. The journal offers you a chance to explore in more detail what the happening meant to you. It helps to avoid the feeling that T. S. Eliot notes: "We had the experience, but missed the meaning".

Some questions that might help you begin to journal:

- What was the experience that moved you?
- What went on in you as it was happening?
- What feelings, emotions or memories did it evoke?
- What stays with you now, as you write, from the experience?
- Is there anything that God might be showing you in all this?

There are also separate exercises, or techniques, that you might want to incorporate into a journal of this kind. Examples would be:

- Keeping a record of your times of formal prayer
- Constructing an imaginary dialogue with God, or with someone important to you

- Working through a question facing you, or a situation challenging you

- Exploring further a significant experience from your past, in the light of where you now find yourself.

A key value in all of this is that you end up with a concrete record "out there", something tangible that you can repeatedly return to.

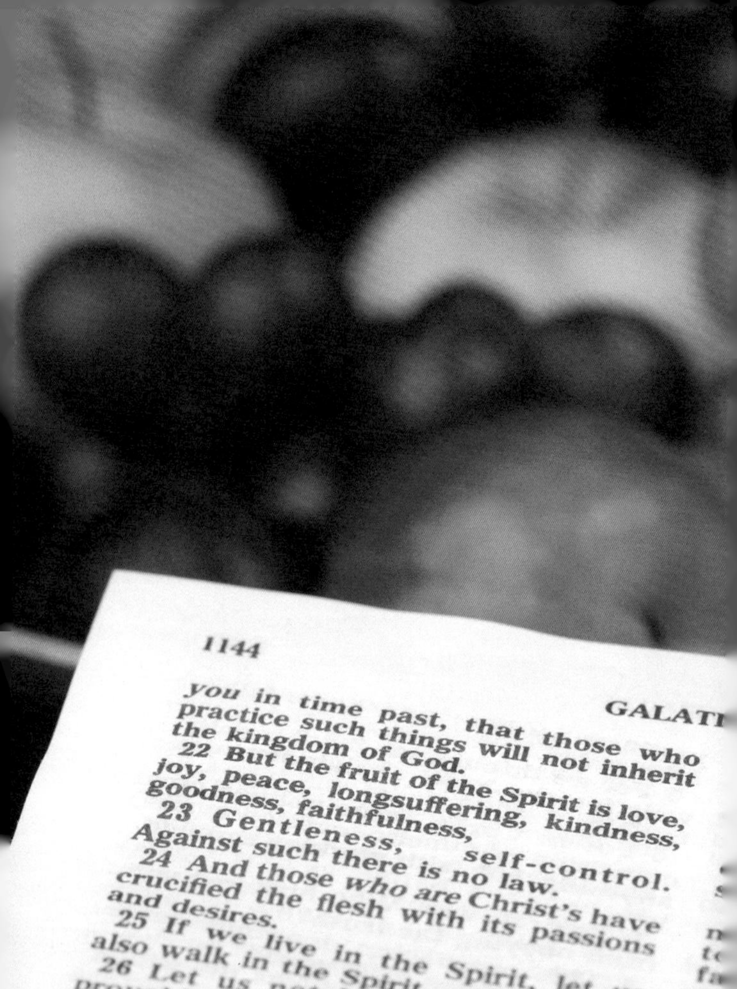
1144
GALATI
you in time past, that those who
practice such things will not inherit
the kingdom of God.
22 But the fruit of the Spirit is love,
joy, peace, longsuffering, kindness,
goodness, faithfulness,
23 Gentleness, self-control.
Against such there is no law.
24 And those who are Christ's have
crucified the flesh with its passions
and desires.
25 If we live in the Spirit, let us
also walk in the Spirit.
26 Let us not become conceited,
provoking one another, envying one
another.

EXERCISE SIX: PRAYING WITH A LISTENING HEART

Lectio divina (Latin for *godly reading*) is a simple yet profound method of prayer found in many traditions of Christian spirituality. Sometimes it is called "meditative reading" or "spiritual reading", but could perhaps better be described as *praying with a listening heart*, since many of the people who have used this approach to prayer throughout the ages could not read.

The "lectio" of *lectio divina* is a listening with the heart, as you tend to do quite naturally when you are struck by the beauty of a sunset, as you are mulling over a treasured memory or as you pay attention to someone you love.

In praying this way you hear a scripture passage or other meaningful text and you let your heart be your guide. You read slowly, with pauses, and relish or drink in the words you are hearing. A natural process takes place: heartfelt listening moves naturally into a deep reflection upon the words and the silences between them; and that deep reflection leads you to some kind of heartfelt response. You find yourself speaking from the heart to the God who has spoken to you.

Let the ease and rhythm of this approach to prayer carry you deeper into God.

Beginning

Choose your scripture passage and become comfortable with it. Read it over a few times to get past any questions that arise about meaning. Invite God to speak to you through the text. Ask for openness. Let yourself settle into an expectant stillness.

This kind of prayer has three "phases" that you move between as you feel drawn: these are traditionally named *lectio* (reading), *meditatio* (meditation) and *oratio* (prayer).

Lectio

Read slowly and gently, listening with your heart to the words. There is no need to rush. No need to get to the end of the passage. When a particular word or phrase strikes you and seems to have some savour, linger with it...

Meditatio

...Let it into you. Pause with it. Let the word or phrase resonate. Repeat it to yourself, relish it, let it echo and soak into you until the "flavour" begins to go, then...

Oratio

...Let yourself respond in prayer, in words from the heart, or a space full of silence, or spontaneous, unspoken feeling. Whenever the moment feels right, begin to read again ...

Ending

When you are ready, mark the end of your time of prayer with some closing gesture or words of prayer. Afterwards you might want to make a note of anything that seemed significant.

Some passages suitable for meditative reading

Luke 1:46-55	*Mary's song of praise*
John 15:1-12	*The vine and the branches*
Romans 8:31-39	*Nothing can separate us from the love of God*
Ephesians 3:14-21	*Infinitely more than we can ask or imagine*
Psalm 139	*Lord, you search me and you know me*
Isaiah 55:1-3	*Listen, and your soul will live*

EXERCISE SEVEN: USING YOUR IMAGINATION

One way God often seems to speak to people in prayer is through the imagination. This can get beyond what I feel I *ought* to think or say in God's presence, what the *correct* ideas to have are. The imagination helps me to see instead what I really want from God, and what God is actually offering me, or calling me to, at this stage in my life.

"But," many people say, "I have no imagination." They tend to mean they don't have the kind of imagination that comes up with vivid, technicolour images. But imagination works in different ways for different people. Some see images with the detail of a film director. Others get a sense of the "feel" of a place, without picturing it in the same way. Others again will build up a mental scene detail by detail.

But no one has no imagination. Take a moment now to get a sense of a place you are fond of, or a person you love. The power that enables you to know what that feels like is the imagination. And the following exercise can help you to use that same power in prayer.

This prayer works well with any gospel or scene from the Hebrew Bible (the Christian Old Testament) where there is action taking place – so don't choose passages that are simply teaching or poetry. One or two examples of suitable passages are given below.

Take a few moments to become still and quiet, and invite God to work through your imagination as you pray with the passage. Ask God for what you want, perhaps "To know you more clearly, love you more dearly, follow you more nearly".

Read through the text two or three times until you are thoroughly familiar with the story. Then let the scene gradually build up in your mind's eye. Take your time, see everything that is around, hear, feel, taste and smell.

Where are you? Take your own place in the unfolding scene. You may start as a bystander, or one of the central characters, or simply enter into the action as yourself.

Let yourself be drawn naturally into conversation with Jesus or another participant. Stay in the scene for as long as you have chosen to, and then draw the prayer to a close.

Some passages suitable for imaginative prayer

Matthew 14:22-33	*Peter walks on the water*
Mark 10:46-52	*The cure of Bartimaeus*
Luke 5:1-11	*Call of four disciples*
John 13:1-17	*Jesus washes the disciples' feet*
Exodus 3:1-6	*Moses and the burning bush*
1 Samuel 3:1-10	*The call of Samuel*

EXERCISE EIGHT: HEALING HURTFUL MEMORIES

Almost everybody has some memories that are painful to revisit. Times when I did something that I know to be wrong, or when someone wronged me. The breakdown of relationships that were important to me, and which it may not have been possible to repair. Times when hopes were dashed, or expectations thwarted. This prayer exercise offers a way to work with these memories before God, in the hope that over time I may find some degree of healing for them.

- Relax in whatever way helps you (sensations of your body; listening to sounds; awareness of your breathing; etc)…
- Allow yourself to become aware of some memory that is still painful for you, some person you tend to hold responsible…
- In imagination see yourself with the person who you feel is the cause of the pain, anger, hurt or resentment…
- Take time to "see" them in a situation which would be familiar to you…

- When you are ready (without forcing anything) say everything you *want* to say to that person. Don't deny or censor any feelings you have…or balk at strong language!
- Go on until you have said all that you can and want to…
- Listen to anything that the other person might say to you…
- The let Jesus come into the place where you are together – talk to him about what you are feeling – listen to him as he speaks to you – to the other person – see him with them – speak to him from the heart – stay with this in any way that seems helpful…
- However you are feeling at the end of the prayer time, and whatever has happened, take time to "say it as it is"…

Healing is a gradual process; you may want to return to this prayer.

EXERCISE NINE: FACING UP TO BEREAVEMENT

The death of a loved one can offer one of the most profound challenges to a person of faith. Why does a good God allow this to happen? How can I continue to pray with confidence to a God who may seem so distant or uncaring? Elisabeth Kübler-Ross identified five stages that people in grief commonly pass through in coming to terms with this kind of experience, including the process of mourning the loss of someone who has been important in your life. She spoke of denial, anger, bargaining, depression and acceptance. While it might seem to be more comfortable to short-circuit the process and move immediately to acceptance, the implication of her work is that each stage here has something to contribute to the process of facing up to the bereavement. None of these feelings are wrong, and there is no set amount of time by which I should have finished with any one of them.

For a Christian, our faith is that God is with me even if I am feeling anger (including anger with God), or depression (so that I cannot feel God's presence). This prayer exercise invites me to sit before God in whatever mood I discover within myself, and to let God continue with his gradual healing work within me.

As usual, take whatever time you need to become still and quiet, interiorly and exteriorly. You might once again like to remind yourself of the different techniques to be found in Exercise 1.

Now become more fully aware of how you are feeling when you remember the person who has died. There may well be a whole complex of feelings. As well as those Kübler-Ross speaks of, there could be regret for things left undone; guilt for wrongs now impossible to put right; gratitude for the good times that you shared together; wondering whether you will meet again; and any number of different feelings. Simply spend some time being aware of them, without self-censorship or judgement.

Notice which of these feelings is, at this particular time of prayerful reflection, the dominant one for you. Take some time to describe it to yourself as fully as possible, as you might do to a close and trusted friend. What is it that you are feeling? What, insofar as you can say, is it that is provoking that feeling in you? What is the result in your own life just now of feeling that way?

Become more consciously aware of God with you in this prayer. You might imagine yourself in the presence of Jesus, who wept at the death of his friend Lazarus (*Jn* 11:35). Take whatever time you need to describe to God, here, how you are feeling. Notice how God, how Jesus, responds to you – with a look, or a word, or a gesture.

Now ask God for whatever you need at this time. It might be the gift of being able to accept your loss. It might be help to move beyond the hopelessness that you feel trapped by. It might simply be a shoulder to cry on. There is no right answer here. Simply make your own request.

If you are able to, before you finish, imagine leaving the person who has died in God's safe-keeping. (At times, particularly when your grief is raw, you might not feel able to do this.) Know that this is a place that you can return to in prayer. And know that God moves forward with you, whether or not you are aware of God's presence.

EXERCISE TEN: GOD IN THE CITY

Imagine that you are sitting on the side of a hill, overlooking a large city. It is night. It might be a city you know, somewhere you've once lived, or where you've had a holiday. Or it might be a place that exists wholly in your imagination. Wherever it is you have in your mind's eye, take a few moments to get in touch with what it is like being there, in the darkness, looking out over the city and its lights.

As you sit there someone comes up to you and says, with absolute conviction: "If you go down into the city tonight, you will find God." They say it in such a way that you know that it's true. What do you feel like when you hear these words? What passes through your heart and mind as you listen to them?

And so you get up and begin to go down the hill into the city. You enter its outskirts, and then move further in towards the centre. You are moving through streets and open areas, past buildings and across roads. How do you go about looking for God? Where do you search for him? Do you involve anyone else in your seeking, ask anyone for help? Or do you search alone?

Take all the time you need to look into all the places where you think and feel that God might be. What are the kinds of places you look at? Who are the kind of people you are searching among? Are there any places or people you find yourself avoiding?

Eventually you find God, and again, you cannot doubt that it is God whom you have found. Where did you make your discovery? What is this God you have found like? Where, and with whom, does he choose to be found?

Spend a little time there in the presence of the God who is to be found in your city, speaking to him "as one friend speaks to another" about what your search was like. Take time to listen out for anything which God particularly wishes to communicate to you through this prayer exercise.

When you are ready, let your attention return to the room you are in, but be aware that you can return to that place in the city at any time, and meet God there again.

Adapted from Anthony de Mello SJ,
Sadhana – a way to God

EXERCISE ELEVEN: REVIEWING YOUR PRAYER

At the end of a period of prayer, it is useful to take a few moments to look back over the time and reflect upon what happened. This is not meant to lead to a judgement that the prayer was "good" or "bad". It is, rather, to come to a deeper appreciation of what went on between God and me as I prayed, and to notice things in the prayer that I might want to return to the next time I come to pray. The following outline may help this review process.

When you have come to the end of a time of prayer, do something to mark the transition from prayer itself to the review. Stand up and move to another part of the room; go outside for a few minutes' breather; make a hot drink. Then come back and allow yourself five or ten minutes to look back over the prayer you have just done.

First ask God to bring to your mind and heart what it would be useful for you to notice in this review. Then recall how you had entered into the prayer. Were you using scripture, or stillness, or praying spontaneously, or some other method?

What were you hoping for in this time of prayer? Did you enter into it asking God for anything, and if so, what?

How did the prayer go? Was it easy or hard to stay with it today? Were you fully involved, or more like a spectator, bored or engaged?

Notice above all what was at the centre of the prayer for yourself on this occasion. Where did you experience life, or light, or energy, where did God seem close? Is there a word, phrase, or image, that captures something of this central point for you?

Were there times or areas in the prayer that you reacted against, which seemed to turn you away from God, or drain that same light, or life, or energy?

If the prayer led you into any sort of conversation with God, what did you say? How did God respond? With a word, a look, a gesture…

Lastly, do you have any sense of "unfinished business" in this time of prayer? Is there anything that you might want to come back to on another occasion?

It can be very helpful to keep a note-book in which you jot down a few reminders from this time of review.

RETREATS

At the heart of the experience of those who took part in the television series *The Great Silence* was a week's retreat at the St Beuno's Spirituality Centre in North Wales. They went to a house were everything (their own rooms, the way meals were served, the chapels and prayer spaces, and even the rural setting) was designed to help them enter into silence more fully and to support them in maintaining that outlook. In addition they were offered the services of a trained spiritual guide, who met with them each day to review the experience, and perhaps offer pointers as to how to move forward. For each of them, it seemed as if this led to some really important results.

There are many centres offering retreat in Britain today. The *Retreats Journal* (which can be ordered from www.retreats.org.uk) lists more than 230 of them, so there is almost certain to be one near you. It needs to be recognised, though, that not all retreats are the same. Some will fill the time with talks or activity. In other places, you will simply be left on your own without guidance. The kind of retreat featured in the programme is technically called an "individually-guided retreat". These can range in length from a day to a month. They are rooted in Ignatian spirituality and anyone who has completed some of the exercises featured in this booklet will find the approach familiar.

The Jesuits run three main centres in Britain offering retreats of this kind. One of the centres is residential, and two non-residential. They are open to people of all faith traditions, as well as those who are genuinely searching for a way forward but without any particular religious affiliation. There are many other such centres throughout Europe and spread across the world. If you have benefitted from the exercises presented here, to make a short retreat could well be a useful next step.

The websites below will give you more details of these centres and their programmes. They will often have printed programmes which you can request. Applications can usually be made either by e-mail or by post.

St Beuno's Spirituality Centre, St Asaph, North Wales

www.beunos.com

This was the centre featured in the TV series. It is situated in the beautiful Vale of Clwyd, 10 miles inland from Rhyl. It has a comprehensive programme of retreats and training courses running throughout the year. The Jesuit poet, Gerard Manley Hopkins, studied theology in this house, and wrote some of his most loved poems while there.

Ignatian Spirituality Centre, Glasgow

www.iscglasgow.co.uk

This non-residential centre was opened in 2007 just off Sauchiehall Street in the middle of Glasgow. A wide range of day and evening events are run in the centre itself, and its team have run residential individually-guided retreats as far afield as Iona and Salamanca. The centre works closely with the Epiphany Group, trained prayer guides from throughout Scotland.

Mount Street Jesuit Centre, London

www.msjc.org.uk

This is a centre attached to a city-centre church in the heart of Mayfair. As well as spirituality, it offers adult theological education and formation, social justice ministries, the full range of parish pastoral services, and a particular programme for young adults. One specialisation of the centre is in running guided retreats in daily life.

Jesuit Spirituality Centres in Europe

www.csloyola.eu/Linky/?lang=en

This site gives access to Jesuit-sponsored spirituality centres throughout Europe, including links to their own websites. All will be working within a tradition familiar from these pages, and a good number will be able to offer guidance in English.

THE WAY FORWARD

The exercises presented in this booklet are drawn from a tradition that has its roots in the experience of a sixteenth century Basque nobleman, Ignatius of Loyola. After a powerful encounter with God in his early 30s, he devoted the rest of his life to helping people discover and work with their own deepest desires, and find out for themselves how following these could lead them closer to God. He wrote a programme for such work, called the "Spiritual Exercises". In it he wrote:

> *Just as taking a walk, travelling on foot, and running are physical exercises, so is the name of spiritual exercises given to any means of preparing and disposing our soul to rid itself of all its disordered affections and then, after their removal, of seeking and finding God's will in the ordering of our life.*

Ignatian spirituality is the name given to the "pathway to God" (as Ignatius called it) that continues to draw on these insights, and present them in words and concepts more attuned to our own times. The exercises here are examples of this approach.

If you want to take your discovery of these methods further, resources of two kinds are listed below. The first are websites that offer further exercises of this kind, as well as material that will support you as you undertake them. If you have made use of the exercises here, you should find the material these sites present already has something of a familiar feel to it. Coming back to this kind of reflection over days and months has a cumulative effect, and the material presented by these sites makes it easy to do this.

The other list of resources is of books that will enable you to learn more about Ignatian spirituality. Now, as has been said above, learning about (the background to) an exercise is not the same as doing it, and if you're pressed for time I would recommend the doing over the learning! Nevertheless some people will want to know more about where exercises like this come from, and how they fit into a wider view of how God is at work in the world. The last four decades have seen an enormous amount written in this area, and the books listed below barely scratch the surface of it. Each, however, has its own lists of further reading, so that those interested can move forward from here.

A third way of taking this process forward is to make a retreat yourself. These can last for as little as an afternoon, or as long as a month. In general, beginners are advised to start with shorter retreats. But the centres listed earlier will be able to advise you on where and how you might start, and fruitfully make your own moves towards *The Great Silence*.

Resources: Websites

www.pray-as-you-go.org

Here you can download, each week, a set of daily exercises presented as a ten-minute mp3 file of prayer exercise using music and scripture. The site also has a variety of other reflective material available.

www.sacredspace.ie

This site will lead you though a guided reflection on a passage of scripture while you sit in front of your computer. It is currently available in over twenty languages.

http://onlineministries.creighton.edu/CollaborativeMinistry/cmo-retreat.html

Here are resources enabling you to make an "at-home" retreat over thirty-four weeks, corresponding to the full Spiritual Exercises of St Ignatius of Loyola. This can be done individually or as part of a group.

www.pathwaystogod.org

This website prepared by the British Province of the Jesuits gives access to a number of resources for those wanting to explore Ignatian spirituality further.

www.theway.org.uk

The website of *The Way*, the journal of spirituality produced by the British Jesuits. Here you can request a sample copy, take out a subscription or download a selection of articles from past issues.

www.theway.org.uk/comersus/store/comersus_welcome.asp
A wide-ranging listing of books on Ignatian spirituality in English currently in print, with the possibility of ordering and paying for them. Most of the books listed below are available there.

Resources: Books

Campbell-Johnston, M., *Time to Change* (London, Darton, Longman & Todd, 2010, ISBN 978-0-232-52782-7). A programme for a series of reflections to be made in the midst of daily life, with the aim of discovering what it is that God is wanting to say to you personally.

de Mello, A., *Sadhana: A Way to God* (St Louis, Institute of Jesuit Sources, 1995 (9th edition), ISBN 978-0-912-42246-6). Subtitled "Christian Exercises in Eastern Form" this influential work draws on bodily and mental exercises derived from eastern faith traditions to enable a deeper stillness and focus within Christian prayer.

Hughes, G. W., *God of Surprises* (London, Darton, Longman & Todd, 2008 (3rd edition), ISBN 978-0-232-52725-4). This modern spiritual classic, which was first published in 1985, outlines a journey inwards to discover the "pearl of great price" that Jesus speaks of in the gospels.

Munitiz, J. and Endean, P. (eds), *St Ignatius of Loyola: Personal Writings* (Harmondsworth, Penguin Classics, 2005, ISBN 978-0-140-43385-2). A selection of writings by the founder of Ignatian spirituality, including the Spiritual Exercises as well as his dictated autobiography and spiritual diary.

Silf, M., *Landmarks: Exploration of Ignatian Spirituality* (London, Darton, Longman & Todd, 1998, ISBN 978-0-232-52254-9). A highly accessible practical introduction to Ignatian spirituality by a prolific author and retreat director. Each chapter concludes with a series of exercises to help the reader make the material their own.

Smith, C. A. and Merz, E., *Finding God in Each Moment* (Indiana, Ave Maria Press, 2006, ISBN 978-1-594-71100-8). A practical guide to discernment in everyday life, focussing particularly on relationships as they enable us to become more aware of God.

Internal Images

Page 8: Walk way, Hallasan mountain in winter, Jeju island, Korea by Pichit Tongma; Page 20: Young woman at home taking notes in her living room by Anatoliy Karlyuk; Page 24: Holy Bible open to Galatians 5, Fruit of the Holy Spirit, Ingrid, H.S.; Page 28: Easter resurrection - abstract artistic religious digital illustration with the figure of the risen jesus by Thoom; Page 36: Aerial view of Christ the Redeemer statue on top of Corcovado, Rio de Janeiro, Brazil by Celso Diniz; Page 44: Saint Ignatius of Loyola, altarpiece in the Basilica of the Sacred Heart of Jesus in Zagreb, Croatia by Zvonimir Atletic.